Pride and Prejudice

by Jane Austen

CEFR level B1

Adapted by Karen Kovacs
for
Read Stories – Learn English

Read Stories – Learn English

Pride and Prejudice: CEFR level B1 (ELT Graded Reader)
Original text by Jane Austen
Adapted text © Karen Kovacs, 2025
Logo © Karen Kovacs, 2025

No part of this book may be reproduced, scanned or distributed in any printed or electronic form without permission. Please do not participate in or encourage piracy of copyrighted materials in violation of the author's rights. Thank you for respecting the hard work of the author.

CONTENTS

What are graded readers?	Page 4
Meet the author	Page 5
People and homes in the story	Page 7
The story	Page 9
Exercises	Page 103
More stories	Page 104
Words from the story	Page 106

WHAT ARE GRADED READERS?

Graded readers are books in easy English. They are written for learners of English and use **vocabulary and grammar at your level**.

Each book also includes some new, more difficult words. There are **definitions** for these words at the back of the book.

WHY READ GRADED READERS?

- Studies show that learners who read in English **improve in all areas much faster** than learners who don't read.

- You **don't need a dictionary** so reading is **relaxing**.

- The stories are all in **modern English**.

- You learn vocabulary and grammar **in context** (this is the best way, according to teachers).

- Reading a book in English improves your **comprehension, fluency** and **confidence**.

- Graded readers are not exercises. They are **real stories** you can enjoy, helping you **learn English naturally**.

Meet
the author

I'm Karen, a writer from England.

I have a Degree in English Literature and a Master's in Linguistics. I've taught English in the UK and abroad.

I speak Hungarian, French and Spanish, so I understand how it feels to learn a new language.

I hope you enjoy this book.

Karen Kovacs

ReadStories-LearnEnglish.com 🌐

Other stories at the same level

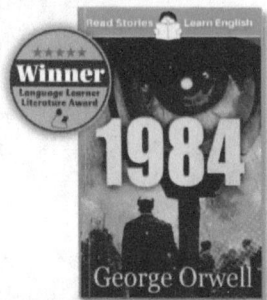

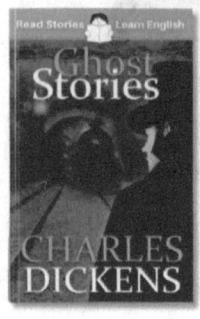

New words

When you see a word in **bold**, go to the back of the book. There you will find a definition of the word.

People in the story

Mr and Mrs Bennet
Their daughters, from eldest to youngest:
    Jane – the prettiest sister
    Lizzy (Elizabeth) – the clever sister
    Mary – the serious sister
    Kitty – who copies Lydia
    Lydia – the **reckless** sister
(Mr) Bingley and Miss Bingley, his sister
(Mr) Darcy and Miss Georgiana Darcy, his sister
Charlotte Lucas – Lizzy's best friend
Mr Collins – Mr Bennet's cousin
Lady Catherine de Bourgh

Homes in the story

Longbourn
the Bennets' **estate** (in Hertfordshire)

Netherfield
Mr Bingley's rented home (in Hertfordshire)

Pemberley
Mr Darcy's estate (in Derbyshire)

Rosings Park
Lady Catherine de Bourgh's estate (in Kent)

Chapter 1

Everybody knows that a single man with a large **fortune** must be looking for a wife.

It doesn't matter if the families in a neighbourhood know nothing about the feelings or views of this man. When he first comes to live there, they feel sure that he is the property of one of their daughters.

"My **dear** Mr Bennet," his wife said to him one day, "have you heard that someone is renting Netherfield at last?"

Mr Bennet replied that he had not.

"It's true," she answered. "My sister has just been here, and she told me all about it."

Mr Bennet didn't reply.

"Don't you want to know who is renting it?" cried his wife, **impatiently**.

"You want to tell me, and I don't mind hearing it."

So Mrs Bennet told her husband excitedly that the house had been taken by a young man with a large fortune from the north of England, who was moving in soon.

"What's his name?"

"Bingley."

"Is he married or single?"

"Single, of course!" replied Mrs Bennet. "A single man with a large fortune – four or five thousand pounds a year. Isn't that fantastic news for our girls?"

"Why is that?" Mr Bennet said. "How can it **affect** them?"

"Oh, why are you being so annoying?" she cried. "You must know that I **intend** him to marry one of them."

"Is that his purpose in moving to Hertfordshire – to marry one of our daughters?"

"His purpose? Don't be silly! But it's very likely that he'll fall in love with one of them and it would be a brilliant marriage because he's rich."

"You're as pretty as any of them. Mr Bingley might fall in love with *you*!" joked Mr Bennet.

"My dear, you **flatter** me. I certainly used to be beautiful but when a woman has five daughters – and the youngest is 15 – she should give up thinking of her own beauty."

"Mr Bingley can marry any of our girls ... although I hope he chooses Lizzy."

"Lizzy is not any better than the others!" answered Mrs Bennet angrily. "She's not as pretty as Jane and not as lively as Lydia. I don't know why she's your favourite."

"None of them are anything very special," he replied, "but Lizzy is cleverer than her sisters."

"How can you talk about your own children like that?" she asked. "It upsets me so much. But you never care how anxious I am."

"You're wrong, my dear," answered Mr Bennet. "I have a lot of respect for your anxiety. It's my old friend. I've lived with it for twenty-three years."

Mr Bennet was a strange mix of things. He was intelligent with a sarcastic sense of humour but he was also generally quiet. After all those years, his wife still didn't understand his character.

His wife was much simpler. She was not intelligent and, whenever she wasn't happy about something, she started complaining that she was anxious. Her purpose in life was to get her daughters married; her pleasure in life was **gossip**.

Mr Bennet earnt two thousand pounds from his small **estate** of Longbourn so he didn't have to work, but the family weren't rich because he had never been good with money.

Fortunately, the women didn't have to wait long to meet their new neighbour. He was at a ball one evening in Meryton, the nearby town, and the Bennets were invited. The young man entered the ballroom with his sister and another young man.

Mr Bingley was good-looking, with a pleasant face and an **easygoing** personality. His sister was **sophisticated** and wore clothes of the latest fashion. However, it was his friend Mr Darcy who attracted the attention of the whole room. He was tall, handsome and extremely sophisticated. Within five minutes, everyone had heard the gossip that he had ten thousand pounds a year.

The men said that he looked like someone you would respect, and the women said that he was better looking than Bingley. The guests admired him for the first half of the evening but then, their opinion changed. It became obvious that he was a **proud** man and that he thought he was better than everyone else there. He became suddenly less popular and not even his large estate in Derbyshire could save him from being disliked.

Mr Bingley had soon introduced himself to everyone in the room. He was lively and charming. He danced every dance, was angry that the ball finished so early and talked of giving one himself at Netherfield.

How completely different his friend was! Mr Darcy only danced once with Miss Bingley, didn't want to be introduced to any other young woman and spent the rest of the evening walking around the room, only speaking to the

Bingleys.

Everyone's mind was made up! He was the proudest, most unpleasant man in the world, and they hoped they would never see him again. The person who disliked him the most was Mrs Bennet and she had a good reason. He had **snubbed** one of her daughters.

Lizzy Bennet had had to sit down for two dances because there were fewer men than women at the ball. During that time, Mr Darcy was standing near enough for her to **overhear** a conversation between him and Mr Bingley.

"Come on, Darcy," he said. "You have to dance. I hate to see you standing around by yourself in this stupid way. You really should dance."

"No, I won't," his friend replied. "You know how I hate it, unless I know my partner well. There's no way I'm dancing at a ball like this. Your sister already has a partner and I couldn't bear to dance with any other woman in the room."

"I wouldn't be as **critical** as you," cried Bingley, "even for a million pounds! I've never met so many pleasant girls in my life as I have this evening, and several of them are very pretty."

"*You* were dancing with the only beautiful girl in the room," said Mr Darcy, looking at the eldest Miss Bennet.

"Oh, she is the most gorgeous girl I've ever seen! But there is one of her sisters sitting down just behind you. She's very pretty too. Shall I introduce you?"

"Which sister do you mean?" asked Darcy, turning around. He looked for a moment at Lizzy until she looked back and he turned quickly away. Then he said coldly, "She's not bad but she's not beautiful enough to **tempt** *me*. And why would I dance with a woman who has been snubbed by other men? Nobody else is dancing with her. You'd better go back to your partner and enjoy her smiles because you're wasting your time with me."

Mr Bingley followed his advice.

Lizzy went straight to her friend, Charlotte Lucas, to tell her what had just happened. Darcy had been rude but Lizzy had no trouble finding the situation funny. She had a kind heart but she enjoyed laughing at people (even herself).

The evening passed pleasantly for the whole family. Mrs Bennet had seen her eldest daughter much admired by the Bingleys. Mr Bingley had danced with her twice and his sister had spent time chatting to her.

Jane was as pleased as her mother about this but in a quieter way. Lizzy felt Jane's pleasure. Mary had heard someone mention her to Miss Bingley as the most talented girl in the neighbourhood, and Kitty and Lydia had been lucky enough never to be without partners, which was all they cared about at their age.

Chapter 2

Later the same evening, the women returned home to Longbourn in a good mood. They found Mr Bennet still up.

"Oh, my dear Mr Bennet," said his wife as she entered the room, "we've had the best evening! I wish you had been there. Jane was so admired and Mr Bingley thought that she was really beautiful. He danced with her twice. Twice! Can you believe it? She was the only person in the room that he asked a second time. He asked Charlotte Lucas first, which annoyed me, but he didn't admire her at all. Nobody can, you know. And he danced with Lizzy once too, and …"

"Say no more about his partners!" cried her husband. "I wish he had hurt his ankle in the first dance!"

"Oh, my dear," continued Mrs Bennet, "I'm delighted with him. He's so handsome! And his sister is charming. I've never seen anything more elegant than her dress."

Here, Mr Bennet interrupted her again and said he didn't want to hear about dresses. So instead she started talking about Mr Darcy, exaggerating how rude he had been.

"But Lizzy isn't losing much if he doesn't like her," she added, "because he's a horrible, unfriendly man. He thinks he's better than us. I can't stand him! Not beautiful enough to tempt him! You should never dance with him, Lizzy, even if he asks you."

"I can promise you, mother," answered Lizzy confidently, "that I will *never* dance with that man."

"He's proud, it's true," Mary said in her serious way, "and that's a very common **flaw**, according to the books I've read. If we are proud, our opinion of ourselves is *too* good …"

Mary carried on talking although nobody was listening anymore. But she didn't notice: she wasn't pretty, clever or interesting but she thought she was all of those things.

When Jane and Lizzy were alone, Jane **revealed** how much she liked Mr Bingley. She was quieter in front of the rest of the family but she was always more honest with Lizzy.

"He's everything I would want in a man," she said. "He's friendly, lively, sensible."

"He's also good-looking," replied Lizzy, smiling, "which a man should be, if he can."

"I was flattered that he asked me to dance a second time. I didn't expect such a **compliment**."

"Didn't you?" said her sister. "*I* did. But that is one great difference between us. Compliments are always a surprise to you but never to me. It was natural that he asked you again. You were clearly five times prettier than every other woman in the room. He certainly is very nice and I give you my permission to like him. You've liked many stupider people."

"Oh, Lizzy!" Jane laughed.

"You're too keen to like people in general. You never see anybody's flaws. All the world is good and kind in your eyes. I've never heard you **criticise** a human being in my life."

"I would never want to rush to criticise anyone but I always say what I think."

"I know you do," Lizzy agreed. "You're being honest – you just don't see people's flaws. Do you like Mr Bingley's sister? She's not as nice as him, is she?"

"Not at first," Jane answered, "but she's lovely when you get to know her. She's going to live with her brother at Netherfield. She'll be a great neighbour."

Lizzy wasn't sure about that but she listened in silence. She had noticed that Miss Bingley was good at making people like her when she wanted to but that she was actually proud and rude. She thought well of herself and badly of others.

"I don't like Mr Darcy at all," Lizzy told her sister.

"I can understand why not," Jane said. "But Miss Bingley told me that he never speaks much in a group of strangers because he's very **reserved**. But he's extremely friendly with people he knows well."

Lizzy wasn't sure about *that* either.

Mr Bingley and Mr Darcy had a close friendship although they were very different. Bingley often asked for Darcy's opinion and followed his advice. Bingley was quite intelligent but Darcy was very clever. He was at the same time proud and critical of everyone. He was sophisticated but he was not charming. Bingley was liked everywhere he went; Darcy was always **offending** everyone.

The way they spoke of the Meryton ball was typical. Bingley said he had never met pleasanter people or prettier girls. And Jane Bennet was as beautiful as an angel. Darcy, **on the other hand**, had seen a collection of people with little beauty and no sophistication. He had no interest in any of them. He did agree that Jane Bennet was pretty but thought she smiled too much.

Miss Bingley said she thought Jane was a sweet girl and she wouldn't mind getting to know her better. Mr Bingley felt his sister's opinion gave him permission to like Jane.

Over the following weeks, the Bennets and the Bingleys saw more of each other. Miss Bingley couldn't bear the mother, Mrs Bennet, and the younger sisters were not worth speaking to. But she didn't mind the two eldest Bennet girls.

Miss Bingley generally **looked down on** people from small country towns like Meryton, finding them unsophisticated. In addition to that, she preferred to spend her time with other rich people – and, although the Bennets were not poor, they were definitely not rich either.

It was clear whenever they met that Jane was falling in love with Mr Bingley. At least it was clear to Lizzy. However, her friend, Charlotte Lucas, didn't see it the same way.

"Jane should be careful," she explained. "She's generally cheerful but I don't think she's making her feelings for Mr Bingley obvious enough. If he doesn't know how she really feels, he might lose confidence. In nine cases out of ten, a woman should show *more* love than she feels, not less, in order to encourage the man."

"But *I* can see how much she likes him," said Lizzy.

"Don't forget," Charlotte replied, "that he doesn't know Jane as well as you do."

Soon, there was another ball. Lizzy was concentrating so

much on Jane and Bingley that she didn't notice that someone was watching *her*. That person was Darcy. Despite his earlier bad opinion of her, he now saw that she had beautiful dark eyes and an intelligent face. And although he tried to be critical, he couldn't **deny** to himself that she had a very good figure and a fun, lively personality. He wanted to get to know her better but he didn't know how to achieve it.

She had no idea about his changing feelings. To her, he was only the man who had not found her beautiful enough to dance with.

Charlotte's father, Sir William Lucas, was talking to Darcy. "Do you dance often?" he asked the younger man.

"Never, if I can help it."

Sir William was surprised by this reply. "Come on, Mr Darcy, surely you enjoy it, like everyone else."

At that moment, Lizzy walked by. "Miss Elizabeth," Sir William said, "why aren't you dancing? Mr Darcy, I'm sure you can't refuse to dance with such a beautiful partner."

Sir William took Lizzy's hand and was about to give it to Darcy, who was surprised but willing to take it. However, Lizzy pulled her hand away and said, "I don't feel like dancing."

Darcy was left alone until Miss Bingley joined him. "I

can guess what you're thinking," she said.

"I bet you can't."

"You're thinking how awful these simple country people are," she said. "And I agree with you."

"You're completely wrong," he answered. "I was thinking how much pleasure it gives me to see beautiful eyes in the face of a pretty woman."

Miss Bingley immediately turned to face him and, looking into his eyes and **blushing**, asked him who he was talking about.

With no hesitation, he replied, "Miss Elizabeth Bennet."

Miss Bingley was shocked and extremely disappointed. "Miss Elizabeth Bennet?" she repeated.

Mr Darcy just turned and walked away.

Chapter 3

Longbourn was only one mile from Meryton, and the young women were usually tempted there three or four times a week, to visit the hat shop and their aunt, Mrs Philips. She always told them the latest news.

One day, she informed them that a **regiment** of soldiers had just arrived in Meryton and they would stay there for the whole winter.

The sisters were soon introduced to the young men, and Kitty and Lydia could now talk of nothing else. After all, the **officers** were handsome and wore red uniforms!

After hearing them talk for hours about the men, Mr Bennet decided that his two youngest daughters were the silliest girls in England. But Mrs Bennet was pleased about the soldiers' arrival because, as she said, "If a smart young officer with five or six thousand pounds a year wants one of my girls, I won't say no to him."

One morning at breakfast, an invitation arrived for Jane from Netherfield. Interrupting Lydia as she was talking about Officer Carter, Mrs Bennet cried, "Well, Jane, who is it from?"

"It's from Miss Bingley," her daughter answered. "She's inviting me for lunch at Netherfield today. Her brother and his friend are eating with the officers so they won't be there."

"That means you won't see Mr Bingley," said Mrs Bennet. "That's very unlucky."

"Can I take the **carriage**?" asked Jane.

"No, my dear," said her mother. "You must go on horseback because it seems likely to rain so you'll have to stay all night. Then you'll see Mr Bingley."

Jane wasn't happy with this idea but she didn't argue.

She went on horseback and, not long after she left, it started raining heavily. Her sisters were worried about her but Mrs Bennet was glad. The rain continued the whole evening; Jane could certainly not come back.

The next morning, a note came for Lizzy from Netherfield. In it, Jane explained that she was very unwell because she had got so wet the day before. She was in bed and Miss Bingley kindly **insisted** that she must stay until she felt better.

"Well, my dear," said Mr Bennet, "if Jane dies, it will be because of your brilliant idea."

"People don't die of silly colds," answered Mrs Bennet

impatiently. "And the Bingleys are taking good care of her."

Elizabeth, feeling really anxious about Jane, decided to go to her. The carriage was not available so she went on foot.

She walked across many fields as quickly as she could and at last she saw the house. Her tights and shoes were very **muddy** but she didn't care.

She was taken into the dining room, where everyone except Jane was eating breakfast. Her appearance caused great surprise. She had walked three miles across muddy fields? They couldn't believe it!

Lizzy could **tell** that Miss Bingley thought she was crazy. Mr Darcy noticed that her face was brighter and even prettier after the exercise but he also thought that her visit was unnecessary. Mr Bingley was kind, as always.

Lizzy was told that Jane had not slept well and that she had a temperature. Lizzy was glad to be taken to her immediately and Jane was extremely happy to see her sister.

Lizzy stayed with Jane all day but, towards the evening, she **reluctantly** admitted to herself that she must go home. However, Jane didn't want her to leave so Miss Bingley, just as reluctantly, offered that Lizzy could stay the night.

A note was sent to Longbourn, informing the girls' parents of the situation and asking them to send clothes to

Netherfield.

At half-past six, Lizzy went downstairs to dinner. Everyone asked how Jane was and Lizzy had to admit that she was unfortunately no better.

Miss Bingley repeated three or four times how terribly, terribly sad she was to hear that and then thought no more about it for the rest of the evening. Mr Bingley, on the other hand, was **genuinely** worried about his guest. He made Lizzy feel welcome, which Miss Bingley and Darcy did not.

When dinner was over, Lizzy returned immediately to Jane, and Miss Bingley began criticising her as soon as she left the room. She had "no style, no beauty and behaved badly".

"Jane is a sweet girl," Miss Bingley continued, "and I hope she marries well. But with a mother and father like that, and no **wealthy** relatives, I'm afraid there is no chance. Their uncle is only a lawyer in Meryton, can you believe it? And they have another uncle who lives in Cheapside!" She laughed as she said it.

Cheapside was a London district that was full of businessmen. Miss Bingley looked down on people who had to work because she and her brother had **inherited** all their money.

"If they had enough uncles to fill all of Cheapside," cried

Mr Bingley, "I would still like them!"

"But your sister is right," said Darcy. "Having relatives in business will reduce their chances of marrying well."

Bingley didn't respond.

The next day, Jane started to recover. In the evening, Lizzy joined the Bingleys and Darcy downstairs again.

Lizzy picked up a book and started reading it. Mr and Miss Bingley were playing cards and Darcy was writing a letter.

"Who are you writing to?" Miss Bingley asked him loudly.

"My sister."

"Oh, dear Miss Darcy!" cried Miss Bingley without any genuine feeling. "Has she grown since the spring?"

"Yes. She's now about Miss Elizabeth Bennet's height," Darcy answered. Lizzy could tell he was annoyed at Miss Bingley's questions and just wanted to finish his letter in peace, but of course Miss Bingley didn't notice that.

A little later, Miss Bingley played the piano for them all and she was not without talent. She suggested that Lizzy should play for them next.

"Oh, no," Lizzy insisted, "I'd rather not! I can't play very well at all."

"That's a shame," replied Miss Bingley. Then she turned

to Darcy. "Your sister plays the piano very well, doesn't she? And she sings too, and speaks many languages!"

Darcy didn't answer her.

As Lizzy didn't want to play, Miss Bingley began again and, this time, played some lively tunes.

Mr Darcy walked up to Lizzy and said, "Do you feel like dancing?"

He had to repeat the question because she didn't reply the first time.

"I heard you, Mr Darcy, but I couldn't decide what to answer. I thought, 'If I say yes, Mr Darcy will laugh at me because he thinks dancing is silly.'"

She smiled, her eyes bright. Darcy looked at her and thought that, if her relatives were of a better **class**, he could easily fall in love with her.

Miss Bingley watched his eyes following Lizzy and was jealous. Later, when Lizzy had gone back to her sister upstairs, Miss Bingley **teased** him about his interest in the Bennet sister.

"After you and Miss Elizabeth Bennet are married, I'm sure you will enjoy the Bennet family's frequent visits to Pemberley. You'll be able to teach the mother to talk less and the younger sisters to stop running after officers."

"Do you have any other brilliant ideas for my future

happiness?" asked Darcy sarcastically, in answer to her joke.

Miss Bingley did and kept talking but Darcy stopped listening.

The next morning, Jane was better so she joined the group for breakfast. Mr Bingley was very kind to her and delighted to see that she had fully recovered. Later that day, the sisters returned home.

Chapter 4

At breakfast the next morning, Mr Bennet said to his wife, "Someone is coming to visit us, my dear."

"Oh, is it Mr Bingley?" asked Mrs Bennet, excitedly. "Jane, you never mentioned it! Why didn't you tell me?"

"It's not Mr Bingley," said her husband. "It's someone we've never met before."

The women were all very surprised and Mr Bennet enjoyed teasing them a bit longer before he revealed to them the name of the guest.

"It's my cousin's son, Mr Collins," he explained at last. "When I'm dead, he will inherit this house and you'll all have to leave it."

"Oh, I **can't bear** to hear him mentioned," cried Mrs Bennet. "Don't talk to me about that awful man! It's terrible that your daughters can't inherit Longbourn just because they're girls. Other estates are inherited by women!"

Jane and Lizzy tried to explain that the situation was not Mr Collins's fault but their mother wouldn't listen.

When Kitty and Lydia found out that Mr Collins was a **clergyman**, they lost all interest in him. After all, clergymen didn't wear red uniforms.

The clergyman arrived later that same day. He was twenty-five years old but not at all handsome. In personality, he was a strange mix. He was both extremely polite and **pompous**.

He had not been with them for long before they began talking about the inheritance.

"I'm sorry that I will inherit the estate," he said to Mrs Bennet. "But I see that your daughters are beautiful so perhaps this problem has an easy solution."

This comment changed Mrs Bennet's opinion of Mr Collins immediately. She now realised that he had come to visit them because he intended to marry one of her daughters. She was delighted because this meant that their house would stay in the family.

"That's very kind of you, Mr Collins," she said. "It's true that, when their father dies, the girls will have nowhere to live."

"Yes, I know," said the clergyman. "Well, don't worry. Lady Catherine de Bourgh has told me I must marry soon and of course she is always right."

"Who is Lady Catherine de Bourgh?" asked Mrs Bennet.

"She's my **patroness**," he explained. This meant that his church was on her estate and she had invited him to be the clergyman there. He therefore worked for her and lived in a house that she provided.

"I'm so grateful to her," he continued. "Lady Catherine is very kind. She's one of the wealthiest women in England with a huge estate called Rosings Park, but she **treats** me very well. Some people say that she looks down on everyone, but I know that isn't true."

This made Lizzy smile because she **suspected** that it *was* true. She also realised something else: Mr Collins was proud and wanted people to think well of him but he was only a clergyman. That was why he talked about his wealthy patroness to everyone, in order to make himself feel more important.

"Lady Catherine has invited me to dinner at Rosings twice," he continued. "Once, she even visited me at home!"

"You're a very lucky man," said Mr Bennet sarcastically.

"Does Lady Catherine have any family?" asked his wife.

"Her husband died a long time ago but she has a daughter. She will inherit Rosings. Unfortunately, she's not very healthy. But I always tell Lady Catherine that her daughter is the most charming and sophisticated girl in the world." He looked at Mr Bennet and spoke more quietly. "I have noticed that women like compliments so I try to give them as often as I can."

"You're right," said Mr Bennet, again sarcastically. "And I can see that you're very good at flattering women. Can I ask, do you plan your compliments in advance?"

Mr Collins didn't realise that Mr Bennet was teasing him because the older man's face remained serious.

"Well, I sometimes write down a few compliments before meeting someone," Mr Collins answered, "but I try not to make that obvious. Compliments shouldn't seem planned."

"No, they shouldn't," replied Mr Bennet. He glanced at Lizzy, and father and daughter exchanged a secret smile. It was clear that Mr Collins was a silly man and not very clever.

The next day, the clergyman began the job of choosing one of the Bennet girls to be his wife. He quickly made his decision: Jane Bennet. She was the eldest and the most beautiful.

However, during a quick chat with Mrs Bennet, he discovered that Jane might soon be engaged. "But my younger daughters are all free," she told him happily.

Mr Collins easily changed from Jane to Lizzy, who was next to her elder sister in age and beauty. Mrs Bennet was delighted to think that she might soon have two daughters married.

Mr Collins kept following Mr Bennet to his private study and talking **non-stop** for hours. This made Mr Bennet feel very **frustrated**. To get rid of him, he suggested that his daughters take Mr Collins for a walk into Meryton.

Kitty and Lydia looked at each other. "Oh, no," they said, **dreading** the walk because they couldn't stand Mr Collins. But they felt immediately more cheerful when they remembered that they would probably see some of the officers in town.

As soon as the group arrived in town, the women's attention was attracted by a young man who they had never seen before. He was wearing a red uniform and was walking with another officer, Denny.

The sisters wondered who he was. Lydia waved at Denny and the two men crossed the street to come and talk to them. Denny introduced them to his friend, Mr Wickham, who had just arrived in Meryton.

Mr Wickham was good-looking and friendly, and all the Bennet sisters liked him immediately. He was so easy to talk to that they hardly noticed Bingley and Darcy riding down the street on their horses.

They came towards the group and Mr Bingley started chatting to them, above all to Jane, of course. Mr Darcy tried very hard not to look at Lizzy. He had realised that it was too obvious that he liked her and therefore he had decided to pay her no attention at all.

Then he suddenly saw the stranger and his face went white. At the same time, Mr Wickham's went red. Lizzy found this very strange and was dying to know the reason.

The following evening, the Bennet sisters, Mr Collins and Mr Wickham were all invited to Mrs Philips's house in Meryton.

Mr Collins immediately started admiring her home and telling her that it was *almost* as beautiful as Lady Catherine de Bourgh's home, Rosings Park. Aunt Philips was a little offended by this, until her nieces explained that Mr Collins had intended it as a compliment because Rosings was a huge house and its owner very wealthy.

When Mr Wickham entered the room with the other officers, every woman looked at him. He was the most handsome, most charming soldier they had ever seen.

Lydia walked up to him and started talking to him in her loud, lively way. However, she soon became interested in a game of cards so he started talking to Lizzy instead.

She wanted to ask him about Darcy but she wasn't brave enough. Luckily, she didn't have to because Wickham mentioned him first. He asked how long Darcy had been in the area.

"About a month," Lizzy answered. "He has a large estate in Derbyshire, I've been told."

"Yes," replied Wickham. "I know the estate and the family very well."

"Oh really?" Lizzy asked.

"You're surprised because we didn't greet each other yesterday," Wickham replied. "Do you know Mr Darcy well?"

"I spent a few days in the same house with him," she answered, "and I find him rude and unfriendly."

"I don't disagree with you," he admitted. Then he explained further. "His father is dead now but he was the best man that ever breathed! But Mr Darcy has behaved very badly towards me."

Lizzy was extremely interested in this story and listened with all her heart.

"My father was old Mr Darcy's **steward** so I grew up on the Pemberley estate," he continued. "Mr Darcy, Darcy's father, loved me very much and he offered me the job of clergyman at a nearby church, where he was patron. I really wanted to accept it but he died soon afterwards. When the job became available, it was given to someone else."

"Really?" Lizzy asked, shocked. "But the father

promised it to you!"

"Yes," said Wickham, "but his son refused to give me the job and gave it to another man instead."

"That's terrible. You should tell everyone about him."

"No," Wickham said. "Until I forget his father, I can never speak badly of his son."

Lizzy respected him for that. "Why did he behave like that towards you?" she asked.

"He hates me. I think he's jealous because his father loved me so much."

"I never liked Mr Darcy," Lizzy said, "but I never expected him to be so cruel. You aren't wealthy like him and he has taken a really good job from you. Tell me, what is Miss Darcy like?"

"I'm sorry to be critical, but she's very similar to her brother – very, very proud. As a child, she was fond of me and she's a pretty girl, about sixteen. But I never see her anymore. She's lived in London since her father's death."

Wickham heard Mr Collins talking about Lady Catherine and he told Lizzy quietly, "Did you know that Lady Catherine de Bourgh and Lady Anne Darcy were sisters? So Lady Catherine is Darcy's aunt."

Lizzy was surprised.

"Her daughter, Miss de Bourgh, will have a very large

fortune," Wickham continued, "and I've heard that she and Darcy will marry one day, **uniting** their two great estates."

This information made Lizzy smile as she thought of poor Miss Bingley. It was obvious that she wanted to marry Darcy but it seemed that would never happen.

Lizzy left the party with her head full of Mr Wickham. All the way home, she could think of nothing but him and everything he had told her.

Chapter 5

As they were getting ready for bed, Lizzy told her eldest sister everything that she had found out about Wickham and Darcy.

The following Tuesday, the Bingleys were holding a ball at Netherfield. Jane was looking forward to dancing with Bingley, and Lizzy with Wickham. Kitty and Lydia were of course very excited, and even Mary said she didn't mind going.

Lizzy tried to convince Mr Collins not to go. "What will Lady Catherine de Bourgh think when she hears that one of her clergymen has gone to a ball?" she asked seriously. "Are you sure that you should go to parties where there is dancing?"

Mr Collins's answer did not please her. "Oh, don't worry, dear Elizabeth. I know Lady Catherine won't mind. Mr Bingley is a **respectable** man so going to a ball at his house won't damage my **reputation**."

Then he took Lizzy's hand and smiled at her. "And may I take this opportunity to ask you for the first two dances?"

Lizzy was extremely disappointed – she had hoped to

dance the first two dances with Wickham. But she had no choice. She had to accept Mr Collins's offer.

To make things worse, her mother had noticed that Mr Collins was paying Lizzy a lot of attention and she made it clear that she thought they would very likely soon be married.

Lizzy entered the ballroom and looked for Mr Wickham's red coat but she couldn't see him. Where was he? She had never suspected for a moment that he wouldn't be there.

Lydia was disappointed too so she asked his friend Denny to explain. "He had to go away on business," he told the Bennet girls. Then he added more quietly, "The truth is, the business wasn't very urgent. I think he just wanted to avoid ... someone here." He looked towards Darcy as he said it.

This comment made Lizzy dislike Mr Darcy even more than before. She was absolutely **determined** not to talk to him that evening.

Soon it was time for the dancing to begin. Lizzy was talking to her friend Charlotte about Mr Collins's silly behaviour when he walked up to Lizzy and took her hand.

Those first two dances were a horrible experience for Lizzy. Mr Collins danced badly and kept stepping on her toes, which made her feel terribly embarrassed. It was a **relief** when it was finally over.

Next she danced with an officer, who talked about Wickham and informed her that he was a very popular member of the regiment.

She then returned to Charlotte and was chatting to her when Mr Darcy suddenly approached. Lizzy was so surprised when he asked her to dance that she couldn't think of an excuse and accepted him.

Just before Lizzy walked away with him, Charlotte said quietly in her friend's ear, "Don't be rude to him, Lizzy. You may like Wickham but Darcy is much richer than him!"

Lizzy went to stand opposite Darcy, with the other couples, waiting for the dance to start.

They stood for a long time without speaking a word and she became worried that their silence would last all through the two dances.

She made a comment about the ball. He replied then was silent again.

"It's your turn to say something now, Mr Darcy. *I* talked about the ball and *you* should talk about the size of the room or the number of couples."

He smiled and promised that he would say whatever she

wanted him to.

"Alright," she said. "That's good enough for now. Perhaps a bit later, I might make the comment that private balls are much pleasanter than public ones."

"Do you always talk then, while you're dancing?"

"Usually, yes!" she answered. "It's better that way. It would look strange to be completely silent for half an hour!"

He didn't answer and was silent once again.

At last, he asked if she and her sisters walked into Meryton very often. She told him they did and then couldn't **resist** adding, "When you met us there the other day, we had just met someone new."

It affected Darcy immediately. His face became very serious and, after a moment, he spoke. "Mr Wickham has the ability to *make* friends very easily. But I'm not sure he has the ability to *keep* them."

"Sadly for him, he has lost your friendship," replied Lizzy, "and it will affect his future forever."

Darcy didn't answer and seemed keen to talk about something else.

"Do you forgive people easily, Mr Darcy?" asked Lizzy and she watched him carefully as he answered.

"The truth is I don't," he admitted. "I hardly ever forgive. If I feel **resentment** towards someone, that doesn't ever change."

"Hmm," she said. "But are you at least very careful not to feel resentment without having a good reason?"

"Of course," Darcy answered confidently.

"You're never affected by **prejudice**?"

"I hope not."

Lizzy carried on. "People who never change their opinions should make sure that their opinions are correct. And they shouldn't have a bad opinion of someone just because that person is less wealthy than them, isn't that right?"

"Why are you asking me these questions?" Darcy asked.

"I just want to understand your character," she said.

"And do you?" he asked, smiling a little.

"Not at all! I hear both good *and* bad things about you, and it's all very confusing."

The dance ended and they moved apart.

Walking towards her mother, Lizzy overheard her talking to Lady Lucas, Charlotte's mother. She was telling that woman all about Jane and Bingley, that she was sure they would soon be married. Lizzy felt extremely embarrassed that her mother was talking loudly of the couple's possible future marriage. It was not a respectable thing to do as it wasn't certain yet. Bingley hadn't **proposed**, after all.

"He's so rich!" cried Mrs Bennet to Lady Lucas. "It will be a great marriage! And it's wonderful for my younger daughters too because, through Bingley, they will meet other rich men."

Lizzy was even more embarrassed when she noticed that Darcy too had overheard her mother's words.

And things got worse. During the meal, Kitty and Lydia laughed so loudly at the young officers' jokes that everyone turned to look at them. Then after the guests had finished eating, it was time for some singing and Mary walked over to the piano. She started playing and singing, very confident that she was doing an excellent job of both. In fact, her voice was weak and her playing not brilliant.

Lizzy looked at Miss Bingley and saw that she was trying not to laugh. Mr Darcy, on the other hand, looked very serious.

Had Lizzy's family all agreed before the ball to embarrass themselves as much as possible during the evening? Of course not, but it almost seemed like that. Lizzy left the ball feeling **ashamed**.

The next day, soon after breakfast, Mr Collins found Lizzy alone. She could guess what he intended to say and dreaded it, but she couldn't escape.

"My dear Elizabeth," he began, pompously, "almost as soon as I arrived in this house, I decided that I wanted you to be my wife. Lady Catherine advised me to choose carefully. She told me, 'Your future wife must be respectable but also not too high class.' Remember, by the way, that when we're husband and wife, you'll be introduced to my patroness, which will be one of the advantages of being married to me. But now, let me tell you how much I love you. I really …"

It was absolutely necessary to interrupt him now.

"Mr Collins, stop," Lizzy cried. "Thank you for your proposal but I cannot accept."

"Ah, I understand you perfectly," he answered, smiling proudly. "When a man proposes for the first time, respectable young ladies always **turn him down**, although secretly they do want to marry him."

"I promise you, Mr Collins, I don't want to marry you."

"You do, I'm sure," he replied. "And don't worry – I won't give up! I'll keep asking until you say yes."

After these words, Lizzy walked quickly from the room, frustrated and annoyed.

She went to see her father in his study, and her mother was also there.

"Did he propose, Lizzy?" asked Mrs Bennet, moving

towards her to give her congratulations. She had tried to listen through the door but hadn't been able to.

"He did, but I said no."

"You said what?" cried Mrs Bennet angrily. "Then I never want to see you again!"

"Elizabeth, you're in a difficult situation," said her father. "From this day, you must become a stranger to one of your parents. Your mother will never see you again if you do *not* marry Mr Collins, and I will never see you again if you *do*."

Lizzy couldn't resist smiling at this, but Mrs Bennet started shouting. "What do you mean? Why aren't you insisting that Lizzy marries him?"

But Mr Bennet wouldn't change his mind and asked them both to leave him alone in his study.

After they left the room, Charlotte arrived to spend the day with the sisters. Lizzy told her that she had turned Mr Collins down.

The clergymen hardly spoke all day, except to Charlotte. She listened to him and let him talk non-stop, which was a big relief to her best friend.

During the day, Jane received a letter from Miss Bingley and she read it to Lizzy. Miss Bingley explained in the letter that everyone at Netherfield had left suddenly. They were all going to London.

"Oh, that's a shame," said Lizzy, surprised. "But you'll see Mr Bingley again soon, I'm sure."

"No, I don't think so," said Jane sadly. "The letter says that they don't intend to come back this winter. And near the end, she writes, 'I look forward to seeing dear Georgiana Darcy again while we're in London. And my brother will also be very pleased to see her. I know he finds her very beautiful.' You see, Lizzy, Mr Bingley doesn't love me."

"No! That's not true!" cried Lizzy. "This is all Miss Bingley's fault. She sees that her brother is in love with you but we aren't rich enough for her and she wants him to marry Miss Darcy instead. She'll try to keep her brother in London and far from you!"

Jane didn't believe her.

When Mrs Bennet heard the news, she was terribly disappointed. She had hoped to have two daughters married before long but now she would have none.

A few days later, the Bennets found out that Mr Collins had proposed to Charlotte Lucas, and she had accepted him.

Chapter 6

Lizzy could not believe the news about her friend. When they next saw each other, Charlotte looked at her carefully.

"I see what you're feeling," she said. "You're surprised because Mr Collins had only recently proposed to you. But I'm not romantic, Lizzy – you know that. I only want a comfortable home and Mr Collins's character is not bad."

"That's true," Lizzy said but without smiling. She could not imagine that her friend would ever be happy with such a silly man.

Mrs Bennet was even more disappointed when she found out. "I can't believe Charlotte Lucas will be owner of this house one day!" she cried. "When your father dies, I'll have to leave my home and watch her move in instead!"

"Don't think such sad thoughts, my dear," said Mr Bennet. "Let's hope for better things. After all, *I* might live longer than *you*."

That idea didn't help Mrs Bennet.

Jane got another letter from Miss Bingley. She and her brother would definitely stay in London all winter. She missed Jane so much! But her brother had important business in the capital and they couldn't change their plans.

Poor Jane was heartbroken and even Lizzy was secretly no longer sure that Bingley loved her. She felt so sorry for her kind, gentle sister.

Mr Wickham was the only person during that time who improved the family's mood a little. They saw him often. If only he had money, he would be the perfect man.

The whole town now knew how badly Darcy had behaved towards him. Everyone felt very clever because they had always disliked that proud man, even before they knew the truth about him.

Mr and Mrs Gardiner, the girls' aunt and uncle, invited Jane to stay with them in their house in Cheapside, in London. Jane was so sad about Bingley and it would give her something else to think about.

There was no danger that she would see Mr Bingley in London. Lizzy knew that his sister and Darcy would not allow it. But Jane thought it was likely that Miss Bingley would visit her while she was there. They were friends, after all. Lizzy was not so sure and thought that Miss Bingley would try to avoid her.

Lizzy was right. Miss Bingley didn't visit Jane at her aunt and uncle's house so, finally, Jane went to see her at hers.

They had tea but Miss Bingley didn't seem in a good mood. It was clear that she was not pleased that Jane had visited her.

"You were right about her, Lizzy," Jane wrote in a letter. "She was trying to avoid me because she's worried that I still want to marry her brother. She **hinted** that he knows I'm in London but is too busy with Mr Darcy to see me. And Miss Darcy is joining them for dinner tonight. She also mentioned that it's very unlikely that Mr Bingley will ever go back to Netherfield."

Lizzy was sad to read the letter but at least Jane no longer believed that Miss Bingley was kind.

During one of their many meetings, Lizzy began to realise that Wickham was giving his attention to someone else instead of her. This woman's name was Miss King and she had recently inherited ten thousand pounds.

Lizzy wrote to Jane that she was not upset, which surprised even her. "My conclusion must therefore be that I was never in love with Wickham. I don't feel jealous of Miss King at all and I'm even willing to believe that she's a nice person. Perhaps this is because I know that, if I were rich, I would be his first choice! But handsome young men need money as much as the ugly ones."

In March, Lizzy left Longbourn to go and visit her friend, Charlotte, now Mrs Collins. She lived quite far away, in Kent. Lizzy was looking forward to seeing her friend again but she dreaded seeing her friend's husband.

She saw the huge estate of Rosings Park first and smiled to remember all that she had heard about its owner, Lady Catherine de Bourgh. Then she reached Mr Collins's house.

Charlotte appeared at the door and welcomed her friend happily. Mr Collins joined her and was perfectly polite, asking if Lizzy's family were all well.

He showed Lizzy round the house very **eagerly**, pointing at every piece of furniture and the lovely views from all the windows. Lizzy smiled to herself. It was obvious that he wanted her to see what she had lost when she turned him down.

"Of course," Mr Collins said, "if you compare it to Rosings, my home is nothing. We are invited there twice a week, so I'm sure you'll meet Lady Catherine soon."

Lizzy was surprised that Charlotte could be happy with this man but she seemed to be. However, Lizzy noticed that, every time Mr Collins said something silly (which was often), Charlotte glanced at Lizzy and blushed.

As Mr Collins had predicted, they soon received an

invitation to Rosings. The clergyman was so excited that he could hardly control himself.

"You'll see," he told Lizzy. "You'll admire Lady Catherine as much as I do!" But Lizzy had her doubts about that.

When she went to change, Mr Collins told her in his usual pompous way, "Lady Catherine won't expect you to be as elegant as her or her daughter because they're a higher class than us and have better clothes. So don't worry – just put on your best dress."

The house at Rosings was huge. They were welcomed into a large room and sat down. Lady Catherine was a tall woman and Lizzy noticed that she had probably been beautiful when she was younger.

When she spoke, it was with complete confidence because she knew that nobody would ever **dare** to disagree with her. She was too rich and too important.

Dinner was delicious and they were served by a huge number of **servants**. Mr Collins complimented everything and Lizzy could see that Lady Catherine was pleased that he did.

Apart from the clergyman's compliments, there was not much conversation. Lizzy was sat next to Miss de Bourgh. She was not pretty, she looked unhealthy and weak, and she never said a word.

When they went back into the other room, Lady Catherine asked Lizzy lots of questions about her family. She answered them politely.

Then Lady Catherine asked, "Do all your sisters play the piano?"

"No, they don't," Lizzy said. "Only Mary. I play a little but not very well."

"Really?" asked Lady Catherine. "Every woman should be able to play the piano."

"I don't see why," replied Lizzy confidently. "People have different interests."

Charlotte smiled to herself, enjoying how brave her friend was, but the older woman was shocked. Lizzy suspected this was the first time someone had disagreed with her.

"You have very strong opinions for such a young person!" she cried. "Tell me, how old are you?"

"I'm twenty-one," Lizzy answered.

Lady Catherine looked at her through narrow eyes but said no more.

Chapter 7

Lizzy began to enjoy her visit. She spent lots of time with Charlotte while Mr Collins was outside gardening. Lizzy had noticed that her friend encouraged her husband to work in the garden as much as possible.

The weather was good for March so Lizzy often went on long walks. She liked to be outside and active.

Easter was approaching and Lizzy found out that Darcy would soon join his aunt at Rosings.

Not long after his arrival, Lady Catherine sent them an invitation and that evening Mr and Mrs Collins and Lizzy went again to Rosings Park.

This time, Lady Catherine didn't talk to her other guests at all. She was much more interested in her nephew, speaking only to him.

The rest of them were complimenting the beautiful piano in the corner of the room. Lady Catherine shouted, "What are you talking about? Let me hear what it is!"

"We were talking about music, Lady Catherine," replied Charlotte.

"Oh, well then I want to join in!" she cried. "Nobody has

better taste in music than I do, although I never learnt to play any instrument." Then she turned to her nephew. "How is Georgiana's playing these days, Darcy?"

Darcy told her that his sister played very well.

"I'm glad to hear it," said his aunt. "I've told Miss Bennet many times that she must play more often if she wishes to improve. She can come here every day if she likes, to practise. And if she uses the piano in the servants' room, nobody will hear her."

Darcy looked ashamed of his aunt's rude comment.

When coffee was over, Lady Catherine invited Lizzy to play for them. The older woman listened for a moment but then started talking to her nephew. However, he soon got up and walked away from her, moving towards the piano.

He watched Lizzy.

"Are you trying to make me feel scared, Mr Darcy, by standing in front of me like that and listening to me so carefully?" she said, laughing. "It hasn't worked because I feel braver than before!"

"You don't really believe I was trying to do that," Darcy said, smiling.

"I didn't think that you liked music," Lizzy said. "After all, at that first ball in Hertfordshire, you didn't want to dance!"

"I didn't know anybody," Darcy said, more seriously.

"True," answered Lizzy, looking up at him, "but why didn't you ask to be introduced?"

"I'm reserved around strangers," he replied honestly. "I don't have the talent that some people have of talking easily with people I don't know well."

"My fingers," said Lizzy, "don't move as easily over this instrument as other women's fingers. But that's my own fault because I don't practise enough."

Darcy understood her meaning. "You're absolutely right," he said, smiling.

Lady Catherine interrupted them and asked what they were talking about. Darcy didn't answer her and Lizzy started playing again.

"My daughter would be an excellent player," Lady Catherine told them, "if her health were better."

Lizzy glanced up from the piano at Darcy and then at Miss de Bourgh. He didn't seem interested in his cousin at all, although Lizzy knew from Wickham that there were plans for them to marry.

When it was time to leave, Lady Catherine said Mr and Mrs Collins and Lizzy could borrow her carriage to go home.

Another week passed. Lizzy was sitting by herself, writing to Jane, while Mr and Mrs Collins went into the nearby village. Suddenly, she heard someone at the door and she was amazed to see Mr Darcy walk into the room.

"Good morning. I hope you're well," he said in a hurried voice. He seemed very nervous.

After she answered, he sat down for a few moments and then got up and walked around the room. Lizzy watched him, confused by this strange behaviour.

After a silence of several minutes, he came towards her and said, anxiously, "I can't help it anymore. I can't control my feelings. You must allow me to tell you how much I admire and love you."

Lizzy couldn't believe it. She looked at him, blushed and was silent. This encouraged him and he began to tell her how he felt. He spoke well but he didn't only speak of his feelings. He also said that she and her family were a lower class than him and that this had made him wait for a long time before proposing.

Lizzy tried to listen patiently – after all, a proposal from a man like Darcy was a compliment – but his words offended her and made her angry.

"Despite my doubts," he went on, "my feelings are very strong and therefore impossible to control. I hope you will accept to be my wife."

When he stopped talking, colour appeared in her cheeks as she replied. "I know that I should feel grateful for your offer of marriage. But I don't. I'm sorry to give pain to anyone but I didn't intend to and I hope it won't last long."

Mr Darcy looked at her and seemed to hear her words with resentment as well as surprise. He was so angry that his face went white. He calmed himself and then said, "Is this the only answer you'll give me? It's not a very polite one!"

"How can you expect a polite answer when you **insulted** me?" she cried. "But I have other reasons for turning you down. Do you think that I could be tempted to accept you when I know that you destroyed my sister's happiness forever?"

As she said these words, Mr Darcy changed colour but he didn't respond.

"You can't deny that you stopped Mr Bingley from seeing Jane when she was in London, and that you have made them both miserable." She paused and noticed from his face that he didn't regret what he had done at all.

"Can you deny it?" she repeated.

"No, I don't deny it," he said proudly. "I did everything I could to keep my friend and your sister apart. Towards *him*

I have been kinder than towards myself."

"There is more," Lizzy continued. "I already had a bad opinion when I heard Mr Wickham's story."

"You're very interested in that man, it seems!" Darcy cried.

"How can I help being interested? You treated him very badly."

"Oh yes, very badly!" Darcy said sarcastically.

"He's poor because of you."

"And this is your opinion of me? Thank you for explaining it so fully. I have a lot of flaws, according to you! It was a mistake not to flatter you and not to hide my doubts. But I'm not ashamed of what I said and I always prefer to be honest."

"If you had flattered me, I would perhaps feel more sorry for you but I would still turn you down," she said. "You look down on everyone and you don't care about other people's feelings. You're the last man in the world I would ever marry."

He was clearly shocked by her cold words.

"You've said enough," he answered sadly. "I understand your feelings and now I will have to feel ashamed of mine."

He hurried out of the room.

Chapter 8

When she woke up the next morning, Lizzy felt a mix of confusing emotions. She was flattered, she was insulted, she was angry. It was impossible to think of anything else so, soon after breakfast, she decided to go for a walk to clear her head.

Lizzy was enjoying the beautiful Kent countryside when suddenly she saw a man ahead of her. She turned away but he called her name so she looked back. It was Mr Darcy, holding out a letter, which she took without thinking.

"I've been walking here for some time, hoping to meet you. Would you mind reading that letter?"

He said goodbye politely and left her alone.

Feeling very curious, Lizzy opened the letter and saw immediately that it was a long one.

"Don't worry – this letter doesn't contain a second proposal. But I believe it is fair for me to have the opportunity to tell you my **side** of the story. There are two things you blame me for:

"Firstly, you blame me for trying to keep Mr Bingley and your sister apart. I'm sorry but I had good reasons for doing it. I noticed very quickly that Bingley preferred your elder sister to any other young woman in the country and everyone expected them to get married. However, I watched your sister carefully and, although she was friendly and cheerful with him, I suspected that she was not in love with Bingley.

"It's likely that I was wrong about her feelings. You know your sister better than I do, so you must be right – she does really love him.

"But this was not my only reason for trying to keep them apart. Your family are not of a high class but, more importantly, they often don't behave respectably. Your mother, your three young sisters and even sometimes your father do not behave properly. I'm genuinely sorry to insult them but it's true.

"I wanted to protect my friend from a close relationship with a family like that. In London, his sister and I explained this to him, but Bingley didn't care much because he's not particularly interested about class. However, he's not a very confident man so it was easy to convince him that your sister didn't love him. We also persuaded him not to return to Hertfordshire.

"Secondly, you blame me for treating Mr Wickham badly. I don't know exactly what he said to you but I'll now tell you the whole truth of his relationship with my family.

"Mr Wickham is the son of a very respectable man, who was for many years the steward of our Pemberley estate. My father loved Wickham and paid for him to go to school and later university, something that Wickham's own father was never able to afford. My father never realised how badly Wickham behaved but I was the same age and more often with him, so I saw it all. He's charming certainly but also selfish and cruel.

"My father was patron of a church and wanted Wickham to be its clergyman. Additionally, he wanted Wickham to inherit a thousand pounds after his death. Unfortunately, both our fathers died five years ago. Immediately afterwards, Wickham admitted he didn't want to be a clergyman. He asked for three thousand pounds instead, which I gave him. Our relationship seemed now to be over.

"For about three years, I heard little of him. But one day, he came to see me, admitting that he had spent all my father's money and asking for more. I don't think you'll blame me when I tell you that I refused. He resented me for it, of course.

"I didn't hear of him again until last summer. My sister was on holiday in Ramsgate with a woman called Mrs Younge, who was paid to look after her. Wickham followed them there. It seems that he already knew Mrs Younge and that she was not an honest woman.

"My sister had of course known Wickham all her life. They now spent long days together and she began to feel that she was in love. As you know, Wickham is very charming so he had no trouble achieving this. He soon convinced her to **elope** with him.

"My sister was only fifteen.

"Luckily, she wrote to tell me that Wickham was with her. She couldn't bear to keep such a big secret from me because we're very close. I'm nearly ten years older than her so she sees me almost like a father.

"I joined them unexpectedly in Ramsgate and Georgiana told me everything. You can imagine what I felt and how I acted.

"We didn't want this to damage my sister's reputation so we didn't tell anyone.

"It's obvious that Wickham was interested in my sister for her fortune, which is thirty thousand pounds. But I can't help thinking that he also wanted to punish me.

"This, Miss Bennet, is the complete truth about my relationship with Wickham. I hope you'll now agree that I wasn't cruel towards him.

"Yours sincerely, Mr Darcy

When she began reading the letter, Lizzy felt a strong prejudice against the writer. She still disliked him for separating Bingley and her sister, and she hated him for his **pride**.

The section about Wickham really surprised her. She didn't believe it at first, but as she read more and more details, her opinion slowly changed. She had thought that Darcy was cruel but, after finding out his side of the story, she could no longer blame him at all.

She saw everything differently and was ashamed of herself. She had always been proud of her ability to understand people but her prejudices had prevented her from seeing the truth about either man.

"Darcy offended me when we first met," she thought, "and that made me too willing to believe lies about him.

And Wickham was charming and flattered me, so I never doubted that he was honest. I thought I was so clever but actually I've been very silly."

She read again the section about Jane. If Darcy was honest about Wickham, then he was probably honest here too. He genuinely believed that Jane didn't love Bingley. Lizzy remembered now Charlotte's words on the subject: "Jane is generally cheerful but I don't think she's making her feelings for Mr Bingley obvious enough."

Lizzy felt embarrassed reading again the section about her family but she couldn't deny that this was also true, especially when she thought about their behaviour at the Netherfield ball. Even her father hadn't acted correctly. He never tried very hard to control his younger daughters. He was happy just to tease and laugh at both them and his wife.

Darcy left Kent the next morning. Lady Catherine felt bored without him so she invited Mr and Mrs Collins and Lizzy for dinner.

"My nephew is very fond of me and will miss me very much, I know," Lady Catherine told the others, with her usual confidence. "He seemed so miserable as he left. He loves Rosings more and more every time he comes."

Mr Collins flattered her by saying that everyone loved

Rosings.

"You're not as lively as usual, Miss Bennet," the older lady noticed. "I suppose you're also sad to leave. When are you going?"

"On Friday," she replied.

It was true that Lizzy was not as cheerful as normal. This was because she was lost in thoughts of Darcy and everything he had told her. But of course, she had to hide that from them all.

A few days later, Lizzy got into a carriage and left Kent behind her. What an interesting stay it had been but what a relief it was to leave!

Jane arrived home from London on the same day, and Lizzy straight away shared with her the surprising news of Darcy's proposal. She also informed her about Wickham but they decided that they shouldn't reveal the truth to others. Darcy had said he didn't want his sister's reputation to be damaged.

Mrs Bennet was pleased to see that Jane was still as beautiful as before but she couldn't help noticing that she seemed no less sad. "Bingley treated her very badly!" she cried to Lizzy. "I hope she dies of a broken heart and then he'll be sorry!"

Lizzy didn't find her youngest sisters in a good mood

either and it was soon clear why not.

Lydia was criticising a hat Kitty had just bought, which she thought was ugly, when Kitty replied, "It doesn't matter what I wear anymore because the regiment has left Meryton!" She looked at Lizzy. "We're heartbroken! We can't eat, drink or sleep!"

"Oh, they've left?" cried Lizzy, secretly happy to hear it.

"They've moved to Brighton," Lydia informed her. "I really want Father to take me there for the summer! I've become really good friends with Mrs Forster. She's the wife of the colonel of the regiment. I could stay with them in Brighton and see all the officers again!"

A moment later, Lydia cried, "Oh, but we have some good news too! Wickham isn't going to marry Miss King after all. She's gone to stay with her uncle in Liverpool."

"I suspect her uncle wasn't happy about her marrying a man without money," Lizzy said with a smile.

Chapter 9

Lydia had already told her sisters that she wanted to go to Brighton to follow all the officers and at dinner she introduced the subject to her father. With great relief, Lizzy saw that he didn't intend to allow the trip.

Unfortunately, however, Lydia received a letter from her friend Mrs Forster (the colonel's wife) the next day, inviting her to Brighton. "Father won't say no now!" she shouted happily.

Mrs Bennet shared her daughter's excitement but Kitty didn't.

"Why didn't Mrs Forster invite me too?" cried Kitty jealously. "It's not fair!"

"I wouldn't want to go," said Mary calmly. "I would rather stay and read my book."

Lydia didn't hear them. She rarely listened to other people and she never listened to Mary.

Lizzy was anxious about her youngest sister's holiday plans and she went to her father's study to talk to him privately.

"Father," she said seriously, "Lydia's so reckless. Please

don't let her go to Brighton. She'll behave badly with all the officers and you won't be there to stop her." Lizzy was especially worried about Wickham but she couldn't tell him that. "She'll give our family a bad reputation and Kitty will copy her as she always does. People will think we're not respectable."

"Don't worry, my love," Mr Bennet replied, smiling kindly and taking her hand. "Everyone who knows you and Jane likes and respects you. It's better for Lydia to be silly far away in Brighton than here!"

So Lydia went to Brighton and Mrs Bennet cried as she watched the carriage leave Longbourn. "I'll miss you, Lydia, but have a wonderful time!"

A few weeks after Lydia left Longbourn, Lizzy left too. She was going on holiday to Derbyshire with her Aunt and Uncle Gardiner. Lizzy was excited and even more so because she was very fond of the Gardiners, who were kind, sensible, intelligent people.

The journey was long but enjoyable. Finally, they arrived in the village of Lambton, where they would stay. Mrs Gardiner had grown up there. She informed her niece that Pemberley was only five miles away.

"Shall we visit the estate tomorrow, Lizzy?" her aunt

asked her one day. "You've heard so much about it. Wickham grew up there, you know."

Lizzy felt anxious. Although it was normal to visit great estates as a tourist, and they had already visited a few others, she was reluctant to go to Pemberley. She might see Mr Darcy, an idea that made her blush!

However, a servant at their hotel told them the next morning that Darcy was not at Pemberley for the summer, so they decided to visit it after all.

The estate was huge and the landscape wonderful. Lizzy admired it in silence as they drove in the carriage. Then at last she saw Pemberley House and could not believe her eyes. It was the most beautiful house she had ever seen.

A servant showed them round, a kind, polite older woman. When they reached the dining room, Lizzy walked to one of the windows and looked out. It was a gorgeous view, with hills, a wood and a stream. She was extremely **impressed**. The views from the other rooms were just as lovely.

All the rooms were big but pleasant and comfortable. "This was nearly my house!" she thought.

In one room, they saw various paintings. One was of Wickham. The servant saw them looking at it so she said, "This young man was the son of old Mr Darcy's steward.

He's in the army but I'm afraid he's very reckless."

Mrs Gardiner looked at her niece, surprised. She didn't know the truth and had only heard good things about the man.

"And that," continued the servant, pointing to another painting, "is Mr Darcy."

"Lizzy," her aunt said, "we've never met him but you can tell us. Does it look like him?"

"Oh, do you know Mr Darcy?" cried the servant and immediately her respect for Lizzy increased even further.

Lizzy went red and said, "A little."

"He's very handsome, isn't he?" said the servant proudly.

"Yes, very handsome," Lizzy agreed.

"He's the handsomest man in the world and the kindest," the woman went on. "He's just like his father, who was a wonderful man too. Some people say he's proud but I think that's only because he doesn't talk non-stop like other young men."

Mr and Mrs Gardiner were very surprised to be given such a good opinion of Mr Darcy because they had heard the gossip about him from the people in Meryton.

When they were finished in the house, they said goodbye to the servant and walked around the huge garden. While Lizzy was admiring the view of the house, the owner of it suddenly appeared!

It was impossible to avoid him now. Their eyes met and both blushed. He was so shocked that for a moment he couldn't move. But he calmed himself and walked up to the little group. Lizzy introduced them.

They both felt embarrassed. Lizzy could hardly lift her eyes to meet his and he kept repeating the same polite questions about her family and their trip because he was so nervous.

Lizzy could tell that her aunt and uncle were very impressed with this sophisticated, handsome man but she only felt ashamed. "He must think so badly of me for coming here," she thought.

Soon Darcy was talking in an easygoing way to them all. Lizzy was surprised that he was so relaxed and also that he was being so polite to her aunt and uncle. It's true that they were intelligent people and she was glad to show him that she had *some* relatives at least who were not embarrassing. But they weren't wealthy. Didn't he look down on them?

She secretly tested him by saying, "Mr and Mrs Gardiner live in Cheapside, Mr Darcy."

She watched his face as she said it, half expecting him to snub them now that he knew which part of London they lived in. But he looked just as friendly as before. "What has happened to him?" she thought. "He's completely changed."

Darcy was eager to show them the estate. They walked around it together, Mr and Mrs Gardiner ahead of them. Lizzy took the opportunity to tell Darcy that they only came because they were told he was away from home. She didn't want to seem rude visiting his private estate when he was there.

"It's not a problem," he said. "Even my servants didn't know I was arriving today. I have some guests coming tomorrow but I decided to arrive early to talk to my steward."

He then explained that his guests were Mr and Miss Bingley. "Someone else is coming too – my sister. Would you mind if I introduced you to her when she arrives? She's dying to meet you."

"So he has talked to his sister about me," Lizzy thought.

The group left Pemberley in their carriage, feeling surprised by Darcy's behaviour but pleased to find him so pleasant.

The next day, they were invited to Pemberley and Lizzy finally met Miss Darcy. Although she was only sixteen, she was tall and elegant. Wickham had told her that she was proud like her brother. But Lizzy could tell immediately that she was just reserved and worried about behaving correctly.

Miss Darcy liked Lizzy straight away. After all, her brother had spoken so well of her and she always trusted his opinions.

Not long afterwards, Mr Bingley came into the room. He was kind as always, and she forgave him straight away for leaving Netherfield. Of course, seeing Miss Bingley again was less enjoyable.

Lizzy watched Bingley with Miss Darcy but it was obvious that there was no special relationship between them. Bingley was a little quieter and less easygoing than he used to be. Was he thinking of Jane as he looked at Lizzy? She suspected so.

"We haven't seen each other since 26th November, when we all danced together at Netherfield," Bingley cried.

Lizzy didn't remember the exact date but she smiled and said he was probably right.

He then asked about her family and, when no one else was listening, he added, "Are *all* your sisters still living at Longbourn?" It wasn't an unusual question but Lizzy understood exactly why he asked it.

Lizzy wasn't brave enough to look often at Darcy but, whenever she did, she noticed that he didn't look proud at all. He seemed relaxed and even smiled a few times, something that clearly didn't surprise the Bingleys at all. Every time Lizzy looked at Darcy, he was already looking at her and they both blushed.

Mr and Mrs Gardiner watched the two of them with interest. They weren't sure of Lizzy's exact feelings and were reluctant to ask her. But it was clear to them that Mr Darcy was very much in love with her.

Chapter 10

One morning, while Lizzy and her aunt and uncle were preparing to go for a walk, a letter arrived from Jane. Lizzy said she wanted to stay and read it so the couple set off for their walk alone.

"Dear Lizzy,

"Something has happened that is both unexpected and serious. Don't worry, we're all well, but I have bad news about Lydia.

"Colonel Forster has written to tell us that she has eloped with one of his officers. With Wickham! Imagine our surprise. To Kitty, however, it doesn't seem completely unexpected.

"I hope we're wrong about his personality, Lizzy, and he's actually a good, respectable man. He must know that Father can't give Lydia any money when she marries so perhaps he really loves her."

The rest of the letter was written the following day.

"I have more bad news. Denny told Colonel Forster that Wickham never intended to marry

Lydia! Wickham and Lydia have gone to London but nobody knows exactly where they are.

"Mother is so anxious that she can't leave her bedroom, and I've never seen Father so badly affected by anything before. And he's angry with Kitty for hiding their relationship. He went to London this morning, to look for them.

"Lizzy, I'm sorry to ask you to end your holiday early but please, please come home as soon as possible. We need you here."

Lizzy jumped up from her seat, eager to find her aunt and uncle. They must all go back to Longbourn without losing any more time.

However, as Lizzy reached the door, it was opened by a servant and Mr Darcy appeared. Her anxious face surprised him but before he could ask what was wrong, she cried, "I'm sorry but I must find my uncle immediately."

"What's the matter?" he asked, looking worried. She didn't answer him. "Let a servant go and find your uncle. You're not well enough to do it."

Lizzy sat down, looking so miserable that it was impossible for Darcy to leave her or stop himself from saying, "What can I do to help? Can I get you anything?"

"No, thank you," she replied, trying to calm herself. "I'm

alright. I'm only upset by some terrible news that I've just received from Longbourn."

She started to cry and couldn't speak for a few minutes. Darcy just watched her in silence, very upset to see her like that.

Finally, she spoke again. "Jane writes to tell me that my youngest sister has run away with … with Mr Wickham. They're together in London but she has no money to tempt him. He won't marry her so her reputation is destroyed forever."

Darcy listened in silence.

"Why didn't I prevent it?" Lizzy went on. "I knew the truth about him. Why didn't I tell my family? But it's all too late now."

"I'm very sorry to hear it and very shocked," Darcy said sadly. "Has anyone tried to find her?"

"My father has gone to London and Jane asks for my uncle to help too. We must leave straight away. But I know very well that nothing can be done. They won't find them and they can't make Wickham marry Lydia."

Darcy didn't answer her. He hardly seemed to hear her and was walking up and down the room, his face serious.

"My family is even more embarrassing now," Lizzy thought sadly as she watched him. "He no longer thinks well of me, I can tell." And in that moment, Lizzy suddenly realised that she could love him but it was too late.

"You must want me to go," he said. "I suppose you won't be able to come to Pemberley today."

"No," Lizzy replied. "Please tell your sister and the others that urgent business calls us home but don't give them details. I know the sad truth can't be hidden forever."

He walked to the door and turned back, their eyes meeting one last time. Then he left.

On the way back to Longbourn, Lizzy informed her aunt and uncle about Wickham's previous reckless behaviour. They were now as worried about Lydia as she was.

Had Lydia always preferred Wickham? No, it had never seemed so. Lizzy was sure that Lydia would like any officer who gave her attention; it didn't matter who it was. Lizzy had to admit too that their parents had not taught Lydia to be sensible and to behave correctly so they must be partly blamed for how she had acted.

They arrived home, and Lizzy and the Gardiners joined the other Bennet sisters in Mrs Bennet's bedroom. They found her upset, anxious and angry.

"Why didn't the Forsters look after dear Lydia better? And now Mr Bennet has gone to London and I know he'll fight Wickham wherever he meets him, and then he'll be killed. And then, before he has been dead five minutes, Mr and Mrs Collins will come and take our house from us."

"It's good to be prepared for the worst, sister," said Mr Gardiner, "but you shouldn't worry so much. That won't happen."

"This is a terrible event," Mary told them all, "but we can learn a useful lesson from it. When a woman's reputation is damaged, it is damaged forever and can never be repaired."

Lizzy was annoyed at Mary for this comment but she was too tired to reply.

Later, when they were alone, Lizzy said to Jane, "Do you realise that we will never marry well now? No respectable man will want us after this **scandal**."

Jane looked down sadly at the floor but didn't respond.

After a few minutes' silence, Jane told Lizzy that Wickham had **debts** in every shop in Meryton. Everybody thought badly of him now and they insisted that in fact they had never trusted him at all. Lizzy didn't believe that.

They found out later that he also had debts in both Brighton and London.

When Mr Gardiner reached the capital, he and Mr Bennet looked for the couple together for a while. Every day that passed, the family at Longbourn waited anxiously for further news.

Mr Gardiner managed to convince Mr Bennet to go back to Longbourn and allow him to carry on looking for Lydia alone.

When Mrs Bennet found this out, she cried, "What? He's coming home without poor Lydia? Who will fight Wickham and make him marry her, if he comes home?"

When he arrived home, he was too tired to speak to any of them for a while. But in the afternoon, he came to have tea with his daughters.

"We're sorry for you, Father," Lizzy said. "You look exhausted. You've had a difficult time."

"Don't mention that," he replied. "This is all my fault so nobody should feel sorry for me. I allowed Lydia to grow up to be a reckless, silly girl. For the first time in my life, I'm ashamed of myself. But I'm not afraid of the feeling – it won't last long."

He took Lizzy's hand. "You were right to warn me last May."

Jane started preparing her mother's tea.

"Oh, your mother is still in her room, is she? What a big drama she's making of this! When Kitty runs away, I'll do the same. I'll stay in my room for weeks and cry non-stop."

"I'll never run away, Father," Kitty said proudly. "And if

I went to Brighton, I would behave better than Lydia."

"Go to Brighton?!" Mr Bennet cried. "No, Kitty. I've learnt to be more careful. No officer will be allowed to enter this house again or even to pass through the village. Balls are no longer permitted and you must not leave the house unless you can first prove that you've spent ten minutes studying sensibly."

Kitty didn't realise her father was joking and started to cry.

Two days after Mr Bennet's return, an urgent letter arrived from London. In it, Mr Gardiner informed the family that Wickham had agreed to marry Lydia but only if someone paid off all his debts.

The family had mixed feelings. They were pleased that the scandal would be over but they felt sorry for Lydia that she would have such an awful husband.

"There are two things I want to know," Mr Bennet said. "How much money has your uncle had to pay? And how can I ever pay him back?"

"Oh!" said Lizzy. "Has Uncle Gardiner paid off Wickham's debts? That's very generous of him!"

"It is," her father agreed. "I imagine that he has had to pay at least ten thousand pounds."

"Ten thousand pounds!" cried Lizzy. "Oh no! That's a huge amount of money."

Chapter 11

Lydia's wedding day arrived. She got married in London and then came to visit her family in Longbourn. As the carriage approached the house, Mrs Bennet looked delighted, Mr Bennet serious and his daughters anxious.

Lydia was still Lydia. She was as loud and confident as before, and was clearly not at all ashamed of herself. Lizzy could hardly bear to listen to her and even Jane was shocked.

"What do you think of my husband?" she cried. "Isn't he handsome?"

Wickham was a little quieter perhaps, but he hadn't changed much either and was still easygoing and charming.

"It's so funny that I'm the youngest of you all but the first to get married!" Lydia said to her sisters, laughing. "We're moving to Newcastle. You must come and visit us. We'll go to lots of balls and, if you stay long enough, I'm sure I can get husbands for you all!"

"Thanks," said Lizzy sarcastically, "but I don't particularly like your way of getting husbands."

One morning, soon after their arrival, as Lydia was sitting

with her two elder sisters, she said to them, "I never told you about the wedding. Aren't you curious to hear about it?"

"Not really," replied Lizzy.

"Well, I'll tell you anyway. We got married at St Clement's Church. My dear Wickham looked so handsome in his uniform. Aunt and Uncle Gardiner were there, and Mr Darcy was there too."

"Mr Darcy!" repeated Lizzy in shock.

"Oh, yes!" said Lydia. Then she put her hand over her mouth. "Oh, I forgot! I wasn't supposed to tell you that. I promised them! They said it had to be a secret! I mustn't say any more about it."

But Lizzy was determined to know everything. She couldn't understand why Darcy would be at Lydia and Wickham's wedding. She went straight to her room and wrote a letter to her aunt in London.

She received an answer very quickly.

"Dear Lizzy,

"Let me explain everything. Mr Darcy came to see us unexpectedly after your father had left, and he talked to your uncle for several hours in his study. He told him that he had found out where your sister and Wickham were staying and had talked to them both. He left Derbyshire only a day after us and went straight to London to look for them.

"He said his reason for helping was that he didn't tell the world the truth about Wickham and therefore felt this scandal was partly his fault. But I believe he had another reason to help. I think you can guess what it is, Lizzy, because it involves you.

"It seems he found out where Wickham was from someone called Mrs Younge, who knows him well. She had previously had the job of looking after Miss Darcy.

"Wickham still wanted to marry for money, which meant he was not serious about marrying Lydia, despite what she believed.

"Your uncle wanted to pay off Wickham's debts, in order to convince him to marry Lydia, but Darcy wouldn't allow this. *He* insisted on paying off all of the debts.

"Of course we're very grateful to Mr Darcy. However, your uncle is frustrated and ashamed that everyone has been told he helped the family when in fact it was secretly Mr Darcy. Your uncle is glad that you at least now know the truth. But please don't tell anyone, except perhaps Jane."

Lizzy was surprised and confused by the contents of this letter. Her aunt had hinted that Darcy had helped the family because he loved her. But how could that be? Lizzy had turned him down in a way that she now felt had been quite rude.

He had seen that she was anxious about Lydia's situation so he had decided to help, without even telling her. This also meant that she could never thank him and this thought made her very unhappy. He had rescued the entire family from scandal but they didn't know it!

As the young couple were leaving Longbourn, Mrs Bennet ran to her favourite daughter and cried, "Oh Lydia, when will we see you again? Newcastle is so far!"

"Oh, I don't know," she replied carelessly. "Not for two or three years, I suppose."

"Write to me very often, my dear."

"I'll write as often as I can. But you know married women have never much time for writing. My sisters can write to *me*. They'll have nothing else to do."

Then she and Wickham got into the carriage and left.

Mrs Bennet was depressed for several days after this but her mood improved when her sister Mrs Philips brought her some news. There was gossip in Meryton that the servants at Netherfield were preparing the house for Mr Bingley, who was coming back to the area in a day or two.

Jane changed colour as she listened but didn't say anything.

"Well, I suppose that's good," Mrs Bennet said, "but I don't really care. I never want to see him again after the way he treated Jane. But he's welcome to come to Netherfield, if he wants to. We'll invite him to dinner."

"Why do you want to do that?" her husband teased. "You promised me last year that he would marry one of my daughters but that didn't happen. Let's leave him alone this time."

Later, Jane told Lizzy, "I saw you glance at me when we heard the news. But I promise you, it doesn't affect me."

Her sister just smiled. Jane was clearly not as calm as she thought she was.

Mr Bingley arrived and, on the third day, Mrs Bennet sent him an invitation. The following morning, she saw him from the window riding towards the house.

Her daughters looked out eagerly. "There's another man with him," Kitty said. "Who can it be?"

"I don't know," answered her mother, uninterested.

"It looks like that man who used to be with him before,"

Kitty continued. "Mr ... oh, what's his name? The tall, proud man."

"Oh, it's Mr Darcy," said Mrs Bennet. "He's a friend of Bingley's so he'll always be welcome here. But I hate him!"

Jane looked at Elizabeth, surprised and worried. She didn't know many details of their meeting in Derbyshire, and therefore thought that Lizzy wouldn't be happy to see him. Lizzy hadn't yet told Jane about the contents of Mrs Gardiner's letter.

Both sisters were anxious as they waited for the men to enter the room.

However, as they waited, Lizzy realised she also felt excited. "If he's coming to the house, he must still love me," she thought happily. She smiled and her eyes shone. "But I have been wrong about him before so perhaps I'm wrong now too. I'll wait and see how he behaves."

At last, a servant brought the men into the room. Jane looked calmer than Lizzy had expected but Lizzy hardly dared look up. After a while, she looked up and saw that Darcy looked as serious as he had been last time in Hertfordshire.

Bingley looked glad to be there but also embarrassed. Mrs Bennet spoke to him kindly but was very cold with Darcy. Lizzy was ashamed to see this, knowing that Darcy had rescued her mother's favourite child from scandal.

Darcy made no effort to speak to Lizzy and she felt very disappointed. "If he came just to be silent and serious, why did he come at all?" she wondered angrily. "I never want to see him again!"

She was pleased to see, however, that although they were shy with each other at first, Jane and Bingley soon started talking together as much as before.

A few days after the visit, Mr Bingley came to the house again, this time alone. His friend had gone to London but would return in ten days' time.

Bingley arrived so early that Jane wasn't dressed yet. Mrs Bennet ran into her bedroom and cried, "Hurry up! He's here!"

When Jane was ready, she joined the other downstairs. After they had all had some tea, Mr Bennet went to his study and Mary went upstairs to read a book.

Mrs Bennet was determined that everyone else should leave too. Then the couple would be alone and Bingley could propose! But Kitty didn't understand her hints.

"Why do you keep **winking** at me, Mother?" she asked. "What do you want me to do?"

"Nothing," answered Mrs Bennet. "I did *not* wink at

you." She then sat quietly for five minutes but, unable to control herself any longer, she suddenly got up and said to Kitty, "Come with me, dear. I want to talk to you."

They left the room, Kitty very confused. Now there was only Lizzy.

In a few minutes, Mrs Bennet half opened the door and shouted, "Lizzy, I want to speak to you."

Jane was embarrassed by her mother's behaviour and didn't want Lizzy to leave but there was no choice.

Mrs Bennet's efforts were successful. After they were left alone, Mr Bingley proposed and Jane gladly accepted.

Chapter 12

Lizzy's congratulations were warmly and genuinely given.

"I'm so happy, Lizzy!" said Jane. "And do you know, he had no idea I was in London last spring?"

"I suspected that," Lizzy said.

"I wish I could see *you* as happy," cried Jane. "If only there was another man like him for you!"

"Well," Lizzy answered, "if I'm *very* lucky, I might one day meet another Mr Collins."

They both laughed.

One morning, about a week after Jane got engaged to Bingley, an elegant carriage arrived at Longbourn. The family had no idea who it was until a servant brought Lady Catherine de Bourgh into the room!

She entered the room in her usual confident way and sat down without saying a word except "good morning" to Mrs Bennet, Lizzy and Kitty, who were the only family members there.

Mrs Bennet was amazed to have a guest of the highest class in her home but sat quietly. Lizzy too was amazed that she had come and could not imagine why.

"You have a small park at the back of your garden," Lady Catherine said at last. "Would you come and have a walk in it with me, Miss Bennet?"

Lizzy **obeyed** and went outside with the older lady. As she was being even ruder than normal, Lizzy was determined not to make any effort at conversation so they walked in silence for a while.

"I'm sure you can easily guess why I'm here."

Lizzy looked at her in surprise. "You're wrong, Lady Catherine. I have no idea."

"Don't tease me!" she answered angrily. "But *I* will be honest although *you* are not. I heard something shocking two days ago. I heard that you will soon be united to my nephew. Although I know it must be impossible and just silly gossip, I had to find out the truth myself so I set off immediately to visit you.

"If you believed it was impossible," said Lizzy, "I'm surprised you came all this way."

"I came because I wanted to hear you deny it!" She looked carefully at Lizzy and then added, "So is it true? Has my nephew proposed to you?"

"You have said that it is impossible."

"Miss Bennet, do you know who I am? How can you dare

to speak to me like this?"

"I don't need to give you the details of my private conversations," Lizzy answered, feeling angrier and angrier.

"Listen!" Lady Catherine went on. "A marriage between you can never happen. No, never. Mr Darcy is engaged to *my daughter*. His mother and I decided that before he was born. Now, what do you say?"

"Only this – that in that case, you can have no reason to believe he will propose to me."

"If you marry him, you'll be hated by his family. We would be embarrassed by the marriage. Your name would never even be mentioned by any of us."

"That would indeed be terrible," replied Lizzy sarcastically.

"Rude girl!" cried Lady Catherine. "I am not used to this behaviour. People always obey me."

"Then you must be heartbroken," Lizzy replied.

"I will not be interrupted! My daughter is of a high class, like Darcy himself. Will a girl like you without fortune separate them? No, she will not! No way!"

"Your nephew and I are not so different. He's a respectable man and I'm the daughter of a respectable man."

"Your family is embarrassing!" the older woman cried.

"If your nephew doesn't mind," said Lizzy, "then why do you?"

"Just tell me – are you engaged to him?"

Lizzy was reluctant to admit it but at last she said, "I am not."

Lady Catherine was pleased and said, more gently, "And will you promise never to become engaged to him?"

"No, I won't."

"Miss Bennet, I am shocked. Are you really that selfish?"

"You have insulted me in every way possible," replied Lizzy. "I will not speak to you anymore. I'm going back to the house."

She started walking and the other woman followed her. "So you refuse to obey me?"

"Your feelings and opinions do not affect me," Lizzy told her.

They reached the carriage and Lady Catherine got in. She turned back to Lizzy and said, "I'm very annoyed."

Lizzy didn't respond. She just walked back into the house.

Her mother guessed that Lady Catherine had come to tell Lizzy that her friend Charlotte was well. Lizzy didn't correct her.

Not long after the surprise visit from his aunt, Darcy came with Bingley to Longbourn. It was agreed that the young people would go for a walk and they left Mr and Mrs Bennet and Mary at home.

Bingley and Jane walked ahead, and the other three walked together without speaking much.

Soon they walked past a friend's house and Kitty said she wanted to go and visit her. "Yes, alright," Lizzy agreed and Kitty left her and Darcy alone.

Feeling suddenly brave, Lizzy turned to him and said, "Mr Darcy, I really must thank you for being so kind to my poor sister. The rest of my family don't know what you did so let me thank you for them too."

Darcy was surprised that she knew the truth but Lizzy explained that she had asked her aunt for an explanation.

"If you want to thank me," he said, "thank me only for yourself. Your family don't need to feel grateful. I respect them, of course, but when I was helping your sister, I thought only of *you*."

Lizzy was too embarrassed to say a word.

After pausing a while, Darcy added, "If your feelings are still the same as last April, please tell me now. Mine haven't changed, but if you tell me not to, I'll never mention them again."

Lizzy explained that her feelings were now completely different.

When he heard this, Darcy was delighted, although Lizzy see this because she didn't dare look at him. He felt happier than he had ever felt before. He was very much in love with her so he responded warmly and eagerly.

They continued walking but without paying any attention to the things around them. Their thoughts and feelings were much too strong.

He told Lizzy that his aunt had visited him after seeing her. Lady Catherine had told him all about her disappointing conversation with Lizzy.

"I know what an honest person you are," he explained, "and that, if you definitely didn't want to marry me, you would just say that. So your answers to Lady Catherine gave me hope."

Lizzy blushed. "Yes!" she laughed. "After all, I insulted you to your face so why wouldn't I insult you to all your relations?"

"What did you say that I didn't deserve?" he replied. "You believed some things that weren't true, but my behaviour at the time was terrible."

"Let's not argue about who we should blame more!" said Lizzy. "My behaviour wasn't perfect either but we've both improved a lot since."

"I'm ashamed to remember how I was," Darcy admitted. "I was selfish and proud, and I looked down on other people. But luckily for me, I met you. And you changed me, dearest, loveliest Elizabeth!"

Chapter 13

At night, Lizzy told Jane her news.

"You're joking, Lizzy. It can't be true! Engaged to Mr Darcy? That's impossible."

"This is a bad beginning," Lizzy answered, laughing. "Nobody else will believe me if you don't. But it's true. He still loves me and we're engaged."

Jane looked at her seriously. "But I know how much you dislike him."

"I don't dislike him anymore. That is all forgotten. In cases like this, a good memory is a serious personality flaw."

Jane still looked amazed. "I suppose I have to believe you. I would, I *do* give you my congratulations but are you sure? Are you *absolutely* sure you can be happy with him?"

"There can be no doubt of that," Lizzy replied. "We've already decided that we're going to be the happiest couple in the world. But are you pleased, Jane? Can you like him?"

"Yes, of course!" cried Jane. "And Bingley will be delighted too. But Lizzy, do you really love him?"

"Oh, yes!" her sister answered, her eyes bright.

"How long have you loved him?"

"I don't exactly know. My feelings have grown so slowly. But I think it all started when I first saw his beautiful estate at Pemberley."

Jane asked her to be serious and Lizzy finally spoke sensibly and convinced her sister that she loved Darcy. She told Jane everything, including Darcy's help with Lydia's marriage. They spent half the night talking.

The next day, Mr Bennet asked Lizzy to join him in his study. When she went in, he was walking around the room looking anxious.

"Lizzy, what is the matter with you? Are you crazy?"

He explained that Darcy had come earlier that day to ask his permission to marry his daughter.

"Haven't you always hated him?" he asked.

She gave him the necessary explanations.

"So you're determined to have him? He's rich, for sure, and you'll have more beautiful clothes and carriages than Jane. But will they make you happy?"

"*They* won't make me happy," Lizzy replied. "*He* will."

"We all know he's a proud, unpleasant person," her father said, "but, if you really like him, I suppose that doesn't matter."

"I do like him," she replied, with tears in her eyes. "I love him. He's not proud anymore. He's a kind, generous person. You don't know him so please don't talk about him in that way."

"My child," said her father, taking her hands, "I don't want to see *you* unable to respect your partner in life."

Lizzy understood that he was hinting at his own marriage, and she was affected by his words. She shared more about Darcy's character and her feelings for him, and at last, her father believed her.

"Well, my dear," he said when she had finished talking, "I have no more to say. If this is the case, he deserves you. I wouldn't want to lose you, my Lizzy, to anyone less **deserving**."

Lizzy then revealed what Darcy had done for Lydia. Her father was very surprised.

"That's wonderful," he cried. "I would have to pay your uncle back but I know Darcy won't accept any money from me, as he's so in love with you."

As she left the room, he said to her, "If any young men come for Mary or Kitty, tell them they're welcome to come in. I'm not busy this afternoon."

Lizzy then went to inform her mother of her engagement.

Mrs Bennet sat in silence at first, unable to speak. Then she cried, "Oh, Lizzy! Is it really true? You're going to be so rich! Much richer than Jane. I'm so pleased, so happy. He's such a charming man, so handsome, so tall! Dear Lizzy, please apologise to him that I disliked him so much before. Three daughters married! Ten thousand a year! I can't believe it!"

It was a happy day for Mrs Bennet when her two most deserving daughters got married. It is easy to imagine how proudly she afterwards talked about Mrs Bingley and Mrs Darcy.

Mr Bennet missed his second daughter very much. His love for her took him away from home more often than anything else could. He loved going to Pemberley, especially when the couple least expected him.

Bingley and Jane didn't stay long at Netherfield. Not even the easygoing Bingley could bear being so near Mrs Bennet for long. He bought an estate not far from Pemberley, and Jane and Lizzy had the great pleasure of living close to each other.

Kitty spent most of her time with her two elder sisters and her personality improved hugely. Now that she could no longer copy Lydia's behaviour, she became less impatient, less silly and more sensible. Although she was often invited to visit Lydia, with the promise of balls and young men, her father would never give her permission.

Mary was the only daughter who remained at home and she had to accompany her mother on her frequent visits to friends and neighbours.

Georgiana moved back to Pemberley and the two women became very close, which Darcy was delighted to see. Georgiana admired Lizzy more than any other woman in the world although she was shocked at first to hear how often Lizzy teased her brother. She never did that because she was a serious girl and respected her older brother too much to laugh at him.

Lady Catherine was extremely angry about the marriage of her nephew. In a letter, she criticised Lizzy so much that, for a while, they didn't see each other. But at last, Lizzy persuaded her husband to forgive his aunt. Lady Catherine recovered from her feelings of resentment, either because she was fond of Darcy or because she wanted to see how Lizzy behaved as his wife. She agreed to come and see them, although she still looked down on Lizzy's family, including her aunt and uncle from the city.

The Gardiners visited often and were always warmly welcomed. Both Darcy and Lizzy really loved them. The couple were always grateful to the Gardiners who, by bringing Lizzy to Derbyshire, had helped to unite them.

THE END

VISIT MY WEBSITE

You will find:
- **information** about my **other books**
- **free stories**
- **free exercises** for this book
  (vocabulary exercises, comprehension exercises and notes about British culture)

ReadStories-LearnEnglish.com

MORE STORIES

A1+ Elementary

A2 Pre-intermediate

B1 Intermediate

B2 Upper intermediate

Words from the story

affect (v)
make something change

ashamed (adj)
feeling embarrassed or guilty about something you (or someone else) did

blush (v)
turn red in the face because you feel embarrassed or shy

can't bear (phr)
not be able to stand or tolerate something

can't resist (phr)
be unable to stop yourself from doing something you want to do

carriage (n)
a vehicle pulled by horses

class (n)
a group of people with similar social or economic status

clergyman (n)
someone who works in a church, like a priest

colonel (n)
a high-level officer in the army

compliment (n)
a nice thing you say about someone or something
(**compliment**, v)

critical (adj)
finding fault with or judging someone or something (**criticise**, v)

dare (v)
be brave enough to do something that is risky or scary

dear (adj)
used to address someone you love or are being friendly to

debt (n)
money that you owe

deny (v)
say that something is not true

deserving (adj)
having the right to something because of what you've done or how you behave

determined (adj)
wanting to do something very much and not allowing anyone or any difficulties to stop you

dread (v)
fear that something bad is going to happen

eager (adj)
very excited and ready to do something

easygoing (adj)
relaxed and not easily upset or worried

elope (v)
run away secretly to get married

estate (n)
a large piece of land with a big house on it

flatter (v)
praise someone too much, often insincerely

flaw (n)
a problem or weakness in a person's behaviour or personality

fortune (n)
a large amount of money

frustrated (adj)
annoyed or upset because you can't do something

genuine (adj)
real or honest

gossip (n)
discussions about other people's private lives

heartbroken (adj)
very sad because of a loss or disappointment

hint (v)
suggest something without saying it directly (**hint**, n)

impatient (adj)
not able to wait calmly

impressed (adj)
feeling admiration or respect for someone or something

inherit (v)
receive money or property after someone dies (**inheritance**, n)

insist (v)
say something firmly or demand something strongly

insult (v)
say or do something that offends someone

intend (v)
plan or mean to do something

look down on (phr v)
think you are better than someone else

muddy (adj)
covered in wet, soft earth or soil

non-stop (adv)
without stopping, continuing all the time

obey (v)
do what you are told

offend (v)
upset someone by what you say or do

officer (n)
a person in charge in the army

on the other hand (phr)
used to introduce a different idea or point of view

overhear (v)
hear what other people are saying without intending to and without their knowledge

patron (n)
someone who helps or supports another person, often by giving them a job or money (**patroness**, female form)

pompous (adj)
acting too proud and self-important

prejudice (n)
an unfair and unreasonable opinion or feeling, especially when formed without enough thought or knowledge

propose (v)
ask someone to marry you (**proposal**, n)

proud (adj)
feeling that you are better and more important than other people (**pride**, n)

reckless (adj)
not caring about the danger or results of your actions

regiment (n)
a large group of soldiers

relief (n)
a feeling of comfort after worry or pain

reluctant (adj)
not wanting to do something

reputation (n)
the opinion that people have of someone, based on past behaviour or character

resent (v)
feel upset or angry about something (**resentment**, n)

reserved (adj)
quiet and not showing feelings easily

respectable (adj)
seen as good or proper by most people

reveal (v)
make something known to somebody

sarcastic (adj)
saying the opposite of what you mean in a way that can be funny or unkind

scandal (n)
something that shocks people because it is wrong or bad

servant (n)
a person who works in someone's home doing jobs like cooking or cleaning

side (n)
perspective, point of view

snub (v)
treat someone rudely by ignoring them

sophisticated (adj)
well-educated or refined

steward (n)
a person who manages land or property for someone else

suspect (v)
think that something might be true

tease (v)
make fun of someone in a playful or unkind way

tell (v)
notice or understand something

tempt (v)
make someone want to do something, especially something wrong

treat (v)
act or behave towards someone in a certain way

turn someone down (phr v)
refuse an offer or request, for example a proposal of marriage

unite (v)
bring people or things together

wealthy (adj)
having a lot of money

wink (v)
quickly close and open one eye, often as a signal

www.ingramcontent.com/pod-product-compliance
Lightning Source LLC
Chambersburg PA
CBHW011958090526
44590CB00023B/3775